Self-Esteem

Effective Strategies For Achieving Success And Cultivating Inner Peace Through Practical Self-reliance Techniques

(The Solution To Low Self-Esteem: Transforming From A State Of Low Self-Esteem To A State Of Unwavering Self-Confidence For A Lifetime)

MauritsLinssen

TABLE OF CONTENT

Taking Advantage Of The Law Of Universal Attraction To Unleash The Magic 1

Developing Self-Assurance In Partnerships 12

Ensure That You Have Adequate Time. 48

Settling In For The Journey Of Self-Esteem 54

How Much Self-Compassion Do I Have? 74

Discovering Yourself 92

Taking Advantage Of The Law Of Universal Attraction To Unleash The Magic

Ella was lying by herself on the weathered porch of her family's New England farmhouse on a breezy mid-July afternoon. With the summer breeze playing the role of maestro, emerald fields, full with tall wheat, danced in a rhythmic manner. The scent of mature grain permeated the air, occasionally accompanied by a whiff of salty sea breeze. A steady sense of longing sank heavily in her chest as the deliberate creaking of her rocking chair acted as the tempo for her thoughts.

Ella had been dealt an unanticipated curveball by life. She had carefully plotted her own path, but a shocking loss had knocked her off it. She was a fervent supporter in taking control of one's destiny and the law of universal attraction, feeling that she was essentially creating her own life's blueprint. She felt confidently that she could attract her greatest wishes to her doorstep by maintaining an optimistic outlook, accurately directing her energy, and connecting with the appropriate frequencies.

But Ella's trust had been shaken when she suddenly lost her job. She found it difficult to reconcile her feelings and ideas with her goals and objectives. There was a precarious balance inside her, one that alternated between holding onto hope and the all-consuming shadow of long-standing fear. Not only was the sudden shift upsetting, but Ella began to wonder how things could have gone so wrong in spite of her strict devotion to values that were important to her.

Ella picked a stalk of wheat as daylight started to part. Her hands were worn from constant use, and the golden grains stood out against them; every crease was a monument to time and endurance. This unassuming plant brought back memories of carefree days when belief in the law of universal attraction was as firm as a rock. The stalk seemed to contain the key to escaping the mental maze she found herself in as she turned it carefully, allowing it to glitter in the setting sun. The question was how she would balance her goals with her current reality.

There has to be a change. Ella sensed a pressing need to develop plans, a fresh road map where transformation and favourable conditions would not only occur, but be demanded. It was necessary to reinterpret the Law of Universal Attraction in a way that was more appropriate for the circumstances surrounding her current situation. She kept going back to her thoughts about her energies, the frequencies she wanted to tune into and the vibrations she wanted to emit, like a lost sailor finding his way back to his guiding lighthouse. Her conundrum was this: How can one turn around when the life they are living barely resembles the life they have always wanted?

The summer sun illuminated the New England skyline in vibrant crimson and gold as it made its departure. Ella sat quietly, basking in the last of the sun's brightness that was now out of sight. Beneath a curtain of twilight, the wheat fields resembled a fretful sea, mirroring her chaotic inner life. As she buried herself in deep reflection in the stillness of the evening, a question started to echo across the enormous space between the sky and the earth: Is it possible to alter the frequencies of our thoughts and feelings in order to change fate when confronted with unchangeable circumstances?

Unlocking Your Dreams: An Exploration of the Law of Universal Attraction

Have you ever had the feeling that something is lacking from your life? As though a vast array of opportunities lies just outside your grasp? It feels like you are watching the world play out like a big symphony from the sidelines, unable to join in on the harmony. Everybody has goals and aspirations, but all too frequently, we discover that these are stifled by day-to-day anxieties, pessimistic ideas, and a sense of disconnection from the lives we really want. However, what if I told you that you could use the power of the cosmos to change the course of your reality?

Here we have the first chapter of "Awakening the Universe Within: A Journey to Rediscover Joy, Love, and Success." Enjoy.

We will explore the Law of Universal Attraction in this chapter, which is a theory that controls how we draw events into our life. Fundamentally, this law says that like attracts like, or that the experiences and chances we encounter are directly influenced by the ideas and feelings we have. You'll be astounded by the Law of Universal Attraction's ability to influence your reality as we examine its concepts and practical applications. At first, it may seem like a fantastical idea.

Understanding how the Law of Universal Attraction affects our lives is the first step in utilising its power. Every idea we have and every feeling we experience emits a particular frequency into the cosmos. Furthermore, like a magnet, situations, individuals, and opportunities that match our prevailing frequencies are drawn to our energetic field. What does this signify to you, then? It implies that you have the ability to design the life you want. You can start to intentionally change your energy and draw good things into your life by being conscious of your thoughts and feelings.

However, how do we tune our feelings and ideas into the frequencies that draw the things we want? Self-awareness and a readiness to accept accountability for our inner selves are the foundations of it all. Building an optimistic and strong attitude is essential since our reality is shaped by the ideas and opinions we hold. This chapter will cover doable methods for rewiring your brain to think and feel more in line with the frequencies of success, joy, and plenty.

The realisation that our external environment is a reflection of our internal environment lies at the core of manifestation. Through intentional creation of favourable situations in our life, we can shift our attention from what we don't want to what we do want. We'll learn how powerful affirmations and visualisation are as instruments for tuning into the frequency of our aspirations. We may change our attitude and allow abundance to come into our lives in all its forms by practicing gratitude and appreciation.

It takes inspired action to embrace the Law of Universal Attraction and materialise your desires instead of merely wishful thinking. You will find activities and useful suggestions in this chapter to help you incorporate these ideas into your everyday life. You will discover how to make intentional decisions that go along with your aspirations and help you get closer to your dreams, from making a vision board to repeating affirmations every day.

We have just begun to scratch the surface of what lies ahead for you on this life-changing adventure as we examine the Law of Universal Attraction in this chapter. This book will immerse you in the energy of the universe and help you discover how to harness your own rebirth potential. By reawakening the universe within you, you will discover the keys to leading a happy, successful life.

Are you prepared to accept the power of the Law of Universal Attraction and live up to your greatness now? Together, let's go out on this adventure and explore the opportunities that await.

Understanding the Law of Universal Attraction, a potent force that moulds our life, is the first step on our journey. According to this fundamental idea, our thoughts and feelings have the ability to draw either favourable or unfavourable situations into our reality. The universe seems to be like a huge mirror that reflects back to us anything we project out into the world.

For a little period, picture yourself in front of this mirror, prepared to let go of its enchantment. You will receive a magnified and amplified reflection of everything you think and feel. The mirror will reflect back experiences and circumstances that increase the love and joy in your life if you emit these emotions. Conversely, if you project negativity and fear, the mirror will reflect back events and circumstances that confirm these emotions.

Developing Self-Assurance In Partnerships

The majority of partnerships present difficulties for those who lack self-confidence. But the focus of this chapter is relationships since, despite appearances, they are more complicated than they seem. Relationships can take many different forms, but insecure people often go in the wrong places to find a partner. Allow me to explain.

Your supervisor expects you to put in a specific amount of work each day. Why do you carry it out? since you are required to do so. But have you ever wondered if the expectation is really reasonable? In order to improve your connection with your boss and avoid leaving work feeling worn out, you should learn a few principles if your boss is giving you too much work, which is contributing to your lack of confidence. The issue arises from others realising how insecure you are. You wind up taking on more work than anybody else wants to, so you have to develop the ability to be ASSERTIVE in interpersonal interactions. If you truly believe that the quantity you are being given is unreasonable, you have the right to remark, "I don't have enough time in the day to do all this."

There are other friend types in relationships that you should consider as well:

companions who adore you exactly as you are

Friends you feel something for that you have lost connection with Friends that make you feel horrible about yourself

Friends who take advantage of you because you let them

pals who share your generosity and are encouraging

You should avoid those who take more from you than they provide. They take advantage of you and make you feel unworthy, and because you lack self-assurance, you allow them to do so. Consider yourself to be a doormat. This mindset conveys that to those who take advantage of you. When you refuse to agree with their requests, they will wear you out and make you feel unworthy. This is especially true if they can assign you extra work or demand more of you than you are willing to give in a relationship.

You must learn to say "no" to toxic friends. Although you may find this difficult at first, once you get beyond your initial feelings of fear, you will feel more confident and whole. The truth is that you feel worn out by these folks since they are time and energy wasters. Learning to say "no" to them also allows you to spend more time with people who value you and makes you feel more content with life rather than exhausted. Make a list of everyone you know and determine which of your pals fit the definition of a toxic friendship—those are the folks you don't need in your life.

The best friends on earth are those who adore you and make you feel good about who you are. You should spend more time with these people. By developing new interests and getting to know people who share your interests, you can also meet new people and form friendships. When this happens, taking up a yoga class or picking up a hobby you've always wanted to pursue will help you connect with people who share your interests.

Lack of information and not knowing what to talk about in social circumstances are some factors that cause people to become timid. Following current events can enable you to develop your own opinions and build self-confidence, both of which are quite beneficial. You can talk about topics that are important to you far more easily when you have opinions about them than when you don't.

Learning to ask open-ended questions will benefit you tremendously in a relationship because it lets others do the talking; but, if you choose to do that, you must have excellent listening skills. You can create a lot of friends this way, but when you do so, you do need to be sincere. By posing straightforward questions and listening to others' responses, you can actually offer yourself some breathing room, which allows you to employ deep breathing techniques to help you relax and pay attention to what is being said rather than freaking out over the social setting you are in.

Reach out to the individuals you are missing. Allocate some time for a conversation or in-person meeting to determine whether these individuals remain important in your life. You will naturally become more assertive the more time you spend with positive people who affirm you or who make you feel good about yourself. This is because you won't be afraid to voice your opinions, which is crucial for those who are uncomfortable in unfamiliar situations. Try to bring a friend to social events where you don't know many people so you don't feel awkward. Then, as you get more comfortable in the social setting, focus on the possibility of making new friends rather than the possibility of embarrassing yourself. Nobody else views you that way, so accepting who you are and refusing to examine your thoughts critically in an attempt to identify flaws are the first steps towards developing self-confidence.

Remember to grin when you get to know someone you are interested in more personally. Always ask questions that invite responses because, once you get past the awkward stage of getting to know someone, you'll feel more confident and able to talk to them without feeling embarrassed.

Consider those you love and know. These might have been people you hardly knew at one point. Let them answer when you are in a new relationship and express your interest in hearing them out rather than listening to your inner voice of fear. You'll feel more at ease and be able to talk with greater ease if you face the world with confidence, head up, and eyes meeting theirs.

You allow these strangers into your life by being empathetic towards them, even though they might be going through a difficult time too. Based on what you discover, you can then determine if these individuals are deserving of your friendship or anything greater.

Be Aware

After conquering powerlessness and anxiety, make objectives for yourself and push yourself to reach them. An increase in self-assurance might work wonders for you and enable you to accomplish your goals. Here, it's important to keep your goals in mind. Being conscious entails being aware of your advantages and disadvantages.

Think about the goals you want to achieve.

Establish goals

And give yourself a round of applause when you reach a goal.

Small joys will inspire you much more to pursue larger objectives. Getting something done is like devouring an elephant. An elephant cannot be consumed in one bite, is it? You must consume it gradually. In the same manner, as you progress along the path to success, set little goals and accomplish them. If your thoughts are clouded or disorganised, just quit thinking about your successes. Pay attention to your breathing and your identity. That ought to aid in your calmness and relaxation.

In-depth discussion of yoga and meditation is covered in Chapter 4.

Establish objectives

In one way or another, we all set objectives to achieve our aspirations, become more successful, etc. We feel proud of ourselves and satisfied when we accomplish that. But occasionally, we have trouble accomplishing our objectives. You get to a "plateau" where it seems as though you are moving backwards or nowhere at all. To proceed, you will need to put all of your newly acquired skills into practice.

Goals should be set with this plateau in mind.

We should practise and persevere till we overcome this.

You want to be precise and able to determine precisely what must be done in order to make things easier to handle.

You ought to conquer your anxieties as well. They serve no purpose. Expand your knowledge and have faith in your own talents to reach the objectives you have set for yourself.

Setting goals can involve everything from generating more money to creating relationships, reaching your goals of being a more successful person, or losing weight—it can be anything that will make your life more comfortable, enjoyable, opulent, or easier. You must first evaluate yourself if you are to meet these objectives.

What is the current state of affairs and why is a change necessary?

What goals do you have and how do you plan to achieve them? To achieve your goals, you must have a distinct feeling of purpose, direction, etc. Once goals are established, achieving them becomes simpler for you.

To achieve the goal, you must possess the patience and tenacity to keep going.

Encourage yourself.

"Motivation" is the one thing that uplifts everybody, even kids, allays anxieties, calms frayed nerves, and encourages them to give their all. People eventually value reputation over money, even if money is the primary motivator for many. Extrinsic motivation and intrinsic motivation are the two categories of motivation. When parents utilise extrinsic incentive on their children, they reward them with toys and presents. Excellent performance quickly turns into a motivating element; this type of motivation is known as "intrinsic motivation" since it originates from inside. In an organisation, this aids in staff motivation. Employees are incentivized to perform to the best of their abilities by bonuses and performance-based pay increases. These elements give employees more self-confidence and motivate them to work harder.

At least until you carve out a place for yourself, the only thing binding your team to you when you manage a small number of employees in a home business is motivation. When Mike started offering home tuition to school dropouts, he found it difficult to keep his staff members. Many of his employees left to work at larger universities in quest of greater financial and social status. Soon after he had trained a number of workers, they would abandon him.

He eventually came to the conclusion that boosting kids' self-esteem was far more important than academic achievement. He called in all of his staff and went on vacation for the weekend. Here, he discussed his own upbringing, failing to live up to the expectations of his parents and teachers, etc. He invited his employees to share their early experiences, the reasons behind their decision to become teachers, and improved strategies for handling challenging pupils. His employees went home with a positive attitude and the expectation that they would have a significant impact on the lives of the kids who most needed it.

Mike convened weekly meetings to examine issues that students were facing and the steps teachers were taking to address them, rather than the cost structure or student achievement. He publicly acknowledged the extra efforts made by each tutor. This inspired the other staff members, and before long, the students thought of the staff as a second family. He selected and trained the greatest educators to serve as mentors and guides for each student in addition to keeping an eye on their academic progress. Of course, the pupils' personalities radiated confidence, and their grades improved noticeably!

Mike then created a novel approach in which students evaluated his staff and wrote a paragraph about each teacher. He was able to determine which teacher went above and beyond as a result. In addition to rewarding the personnel, he named the teacher in public. He turned it into a place of learning where, in addition to academics, life lessons and moral principles could be freely taught to both students and teachers.

Simple encouragement, asking even the lowest-ranking employee for advice, finding out about their family and working out common issues, taking a day off to enjoy a drink, and going on vacation with their family are all motivating factors, even though initially rewarding staff financially may not be feasible. When we start a task or a job, we ask ourselves, "What's in it for me?" fostering a culture of trust and unity aids in reassuring employees that they will soon receive a fair wage. Ensuring transparency in the accounting system also prevents people from feeling deceived.

When your employees feel valued and like they belong, they will stick with your business despite outside pressure. In the end, any firm wants to build goodwill among its employees as well as among its consumers in addition to making a profit. Any firm that wants to succeed needs assistance from people around it.

The individual schedule

Establish a daily practice of Rebirthing for yourself. Breathwork demands self-control and dedication. Let's look at some pointers to assist you in creating a consistent, growing practice.

1. Establish definite objectives

Establish the objectives you hope to accomplish with RebirthingBreathwork. These objectives might deal with lowering tension, mending broken hearts, developing oneself, or other particular advantages.

2. Begin with brief meetings.

Start with shorter sessions if you are new to rebirthing, like 10 to 20 minutes. You'll be able to adjust to the exercise and gain a greater understanding of how your body and mind react as a result.

3. Create a consistent timetable

Select a period of time during the day when you can practise uninterrupted. Either in the morning when you wake up or in the evening right before bed. A routine can be established by adhering to a set schedule.

4. Establish a nurturing atmosphere

Locate a peaceful, quiet area where you may practise without interruptions. You might dedicate a particular area of your house to the Rebirthing practice.

5. Progression and Graduality

Over time, progressively extend the duration of your sessions. Depending on your needs and capabilities, you can extend the practice to 30 minutes, 40 minutes, or longer if you become comfortable with it.

6. Maintain a journal

After every session, record your experiences, emotions, and thoughts in a journal. This will assist you in monitoring your development, arising emotions, and changes that you are going through.

7. Groups or a guide

It can be beneficial to attend classes taught by a licenced professional or seasoned instructor, particularly in the beginning. Joining practice groups can also provide you with support and an opportunity to share experiences.

8. Remain dependable

In any endeavour, constancy is essential. Try to maintain a consistent practice schedule at least two or three times a week, even if you are unable to practice daily. This will enhance the experience and help to consolidate the advantages.

9. Pay attention to your physical needs

Keep in mind that Rebirthing should be a comfortable and enjoyable exercise. Practice at a slower pace or cease altogether if a session is making you feel too tense or uneasy. Pay attention to your body's cues and honour them.

10. Adjust the exercise to your need.

You can customise the Rebirthing process to suit your interests and needs.

Try with various breathing techniques, such adding pauses or slightly altering the pattern, to see what suits you the best.

Carry Out the Conversation

It makes a lot of sense to dress the part you wish to play if you don't feel secure yet. Consider the "you" that you pictured in the first stage, then act on that vision. Pay attention to your posture—the higher you stand, the more confident you'll feel—dress in a way that makes you feel like a movie star (this might vary depending on what feels good to you!), and speak clearly and confidently.

A happy and productive existence requires having strong self-esteem and confidence, but as we've already established, these qualities are not always simple to achieve. Gaining self-esteem and confidence can be a protracted and challenging process for many women. But seeming to be confident and self-assured can be a good method to get things started and eventually turn into a reality.

The notion that our ideas, emotions, and behaviours are interrelated is the foundation of the concept of pretending to be confident. Over time, genuine changes in our thoughts and emotions can result from our ability to deceive our brain into thinking and feeling more confident through our actions. We can end the vicious cycle of negative thinking and poor self-esteem by pretending to be confident, and then we can start laying the groundwork for genuine confidence and high self-esteem.

The ability to conquer our anxieties and doubts is one of the main advantages of pretending to be confident. Even when we don't feel confident, when we act confidently, we face our concerns head-on and take action. This can support us in overcoming our limiting beliefs and developing resilience. Furthermore, we can develop new neural pathways in our brains linked with confidence by pretending to be confident. This will facilitate the recollection and execution of confident behaviours in the future.

Faking confidence also has the virtue of enhancing our perception of ourselves. People see us as confident when we project confidence, and this can enhance our sense of self and increase our self-worth. Moreover, we are more inclined to take care of ourselves and make positive life changes when we feel good about ourselves.

Long-term benefits of pretending to be confident include the development of genuine confidence and good self-esteem that can result from this practice. We will grow more at ease with taking chances and venturing outside of our comfort zones as long as we keep up our façade of confidence and take on difficulties. This can assist us in gaining the knowledge and expertise required to truly gain confidence and a high sense of self-worth.

Monitoring Your Development

Maintaining momentum and making sure you stay on track to reach your goals require tracking your progress. Here's how to monitor your development efficiently:

1. Keep a Journal or Planner: You can track your daily or weekly progress with the aid of a planner or journal. Keep a record of your actions, accomplishments, and difficulties.

2. Establish benchmarks: Divide your objectives into manageable checkpoints. Milestones are particular junctures in the journey that indicate your advancement. As you accomplish each goal, keep track of your accomplishments.

3. Make Use of Technology: There are lots of applications and online resources for tracking goals. They can support your organisation, progress tracking, and reminder setting.

4. Make a Progress Chart: Use a graph or chart to show your progress. This graphic depiction can inspire you and show you how far you've come.

5. Review Often: Make time to go over your efforts on a frequent basis. This can be a weekly or monthly routine when you evaluate your progress and make any required corrections.

6. Modify Your Objectives as Needed: Situations can alter or you may find that your original objectives are no longer applicable. Don't be afraid to modify your objectives as needed. Setting goals that are effective requires flexibility.

7. Honour accomplishments: Honour all of your accomplishments, no matter how modest. Recognising your accomplishments strengthens a positive outlook and increases drive.

8. Keep Your Focus: Remain committed to your objectives and stay away from distractions that could impede your success. Sort your tasks according to

how they will help you achieve your objectives.

Honouring Your Achievements

Setting goals requires you to celebrate your accomplishments. It strengthens a positive outlook, raises self-esteem, and inspires one to pursue new goals. How to Celebrate Your Achievements:

1. Celebrate Your Success: Give yourself a moment to celebrate and appreciate your accomplishments. Give yourself credit for any accomplishments, no matter how big or small.

2. Show Your Gratitude: Thank you for all of your accomplishments. Acknowledge the assistance that others have provided for you during your journey.

3. Give Yourself a Treat: Give yourself a well-earned treat. It might be a tiny luxury, a unique encounter, or anything that holds personal significance for you.

4. Share Your Success: Tell your loved ones and friends about your accomplishments. Joining people in celebration might make you happier and foster a sense of community.

5. Consider Your Journey: Give some thought to the lessons you've discovered along the way. Think on the ways in which your perseverance, attitude, and resilience helped you succeed.

6. Set New Objectives: To continue your path of development and accomplishment, set new objectives once you've celebrated a victory. Being successful is an ongoing journey.

7. Preserve Humility: It's vital to celebrate accomplishments, but it's also important to preserve humility. Acknowledge that obstacles and disappointments are common to success and maintain your modesty despite your accomplishments.

8. Pay It Forward: Think about ways you may help others by using your success. It

can be really satisfying to pay it forward by imparting your expertise or encouraging others to pursue their goals.

To sum up, developing and achieving goals is essential to adopting the proper mindset, achieving success, and finding happiness. To turn dreams into reality, it's important to track progress, set clear goals, remain motivated, and celebrate accomplishments. Keep in mind that your attitude is what propels you forward as you implement these ideas to your life. You can reach your greatest potential and realise your aspirations if you have an optimistic outlook, establish realistic goals, and persevere through life.

Reduce your worry.

You lose all of your energy when you worry. It undermines your efforts, depletes your optimism, and overwhelms you. The best kind of self-sabotage! Thinking on helpful rather than destructive activities is one way to approach this. Financial difficulties won't go away if they are causing you to lose sleep. Rather, devise a plan for handling problems, enlist the assistance of a friend or professional, find ways to make things better, and take the initiative. Even if you won't be able to address every problem in a day, you will undoubtedly get a better night's sleep.

Take a moment to relax.

You're not feeling well, then. Put that in perspective; it's only one among thousands, so don't give it more weight than it warrants. You are not characterised by a bad day or any other day; rather, you are the complete package, strengths and weaknesses included. Honour your prior successes and the obstacles you overcome to get to where you are today. Why not accept a compliment? Take some time to pamper yourself; go out to dinner, have a long hot bath, or do anything else that makes your day more enjoyable. One negative experience does not have to force you to suffer or descend into self-pity.

Be truthful.

The constant need to win others over is incredibly alluring since it gives us a sense of acceptance, love, and appreciation. But you turn into a doormat when it conflicts with your own desires. Saying "no" when others want you to say "yes" is totally acceptable. The next time your friend wants to pick her up from the train station and you have decided to stay in and relax, just tell her that while it is very much appreciated, you have other commitments. Use your "no" more frequently, without feeling guilty, as it upholds your self-worth.

Make a statement for yourself

The idea that powerful women are haughty and domineering is an urban legend. Even when someone deserves to be in the spotlight, such qualities are sufficient to keep them out of it. Don't be embarrassed to showcase your abilities, accomplishments, and skills. Do it if it requires making a statement, standing up, or speaking up. Maintain your composure and face challenges head-on, confident in your understanding of the subject matter. Being assertive is not being forceful; the more you practise it, the more in control you will feel.

Release the urges within you

Get in touch with your deepest wants and ask yourself honestly what you want in a personal, professional, and sexual sense. Storing things behind closed doors is akin to purchasing an elegant new gown that you never wear because you don't want to draw attention to yourself. Just as your desires, which are all valid aspects of who you are, will sit in your wardrobe and accumulate dust, so too will that garment. Without feeling the need to defend them, embrace, express, and pursue them. You deserve so much more in life, and if you don't, you'll always feel trapped and constricted.

More time spent with the people you love

You are undoubtedly a one-woman show, but you will find much more balance in your life if you talk to friends, family, or trusted peers about your struggles. Everyone requires assistance from time to time, whether it be professional, psychological, or emotional. You may believe that isolating yourself and trying to handle things alone is a safe approach since it keeps you protected. In actuality, your self-defeating behaviour has persuaded you to believe that you can handle difficulties on your own. You all need each other, so reach out and spend some time with your female pals.

Avoid undermining people.

Nothing is worse than demeaning other women, and if you engage in this behaviour, consider the implications for your own fears. You shouldn't undermine other people's attempts to achieve the same degree of success as you, even if you have worked hard to get where you are in life. You won't gain any brownie points for being patronising or condescending, and you won't gain any respect or affection either. Remind yourself that you have had a difficult time, and whenever you can, lend a helping hand to others. That is a really powerful way to live.

Identify your triggers.

By observing the things that set off those self-defeating patterns, you can learn to identify them. Consider what is causing you to act in a way that is detrimental to yourself because you are stressed out. It may be something as simple as your partner's irate tone, which causes you to become defensive even when it's not aimed at you. There are two possible reasons for this: either you're scared, or you're bored and your mind starts to wander (there's always a chance of recycling harmful thoughts when that happens). When you are under stress, self-doubt might surface, and even when things are going well, imposter syndrome can strike.

Keeping a daily journal is something I would recommend as a helpful practice to help you get over your self-sabotaging behaviour. Writing down your feelings and thoughts can have a significant impact. You will be astounded at how much clarity you can gain from it, in addition to the fact that it is a purifying procedure during which you release all of your worries and uncertainties. When I was younger, I kept a diary that served as a kind of confidante. It was always easier for me to understand where I had overreacted and when I had been justified when I went back and looked at what I had written. During my adolescent years, it served as an emotional compass for me. After that, I gave up the habit permanently.

Ensure That You Have Adequate Time.

Just telling yourself, "I don't have the time," is a common way to lose motivation, fail to stick to your strategy, and miss your target. It makes sense—we all lead hectic lives with obligations and other concerns that take up our time, sometimes without our knowledge. You can take a few steps to lessen the issue and eventually get proficient with it.

Utilise your journal first. It's useful for organising your routine, week, and even day in addition to expressing yourself and writing down your goals. Write down the times you are available; don't be too ambitious at first; remember, gradual change is simpler to implement. Your chances of success will be enhanced if you do this. According to an old proverb, you should reheat water very slowly before boiling a frog since he won't realise until it's too late. If you immediately raise the temperature, he will just leap out.

Try organising things like your study materials ahead of time to save time if you have a time-consuming goal, like a writing assignment or a tough fitness regimen. Making preparations ahead of time will greatly you in making the most use of your time.

Step two is to rise early. or before it's too late! Regardless of the day or your schedule, get out of bed and move by nine in the morning. You'll feel like you've got a good start to the day and your subconscious will get the message that you're prepared to take on the day. If you have to go for work, you may plan an hour on your calendar for a workout, a lesson, or some work on your project before you leave. But being able to wake up early enough is a prerequisite for it!

Take a nap!

In keeping with the goal of rising from bed at a decent hour, numerous studies have demonstrated the critical importance of a restful night's sleep for optimal physical and mental well-being. In addition, getting too little sleep will make you depressed and give you less mental stamina, which is what you need to strengthen your resolve. Thus, aim for no less than 7 hours each night. Eight hours is preferable! Some experts believe that humans are predisposed to wake up at sunrise and go to bed at night because of our ancestors, although that may be pushing it given the modern environment we live in! However, the idea is sound. There are a few things that can help if you have the contemporary ailment of insomnia, or trouble falling asleep:

In the hour before going to bed, avoid watching TV or using the internet. It will be harder for you to relax because of the overstimulation and confusion caused by the light and visual stimulation of the screen or devices. Your body will begin to think that it is still daylight. Start lowering the lights an hour before going to bed using the same method. It comes down to developing a schedule and a "bedtime routine," as was previously mentioned.

Try to avoid using your bedroom for hobbies like watching TV, browsing the internet, studying, or other things. Make an effort to keep the bedroom for sleeping.

Steer clear of caffeine and alcohol right before bed. Both alcohol and caffeine are known to lower the quality of your sleep. Additionally, refrain from eating or exercising two hours before bed.

Try to de-stress before bed by watching the news earlier in the evening to avoid its relentless negativity, and try to avoid arguments and emotional upheavals as much as you can.

Refuse Negative Thoughts and Maintain Your Focus!

Recognise that you will occasionally experience unpleasant thoughts, such as feelings of boredom, irritation, or pessimism.

You could teach your mind to focus on other things as a solution. Give your negative thoughts a trigger action, such as some exercise, your favourite upbeat song, or another pastime. And in the event that you are unable to do so, consider anything enjoyable. It might be a humorous scene from a comedy show or a fond memory. This places you in control of your ideas. Keep in mind that our thoughts influence our behaviours and actions.

Settling In For The Journey Of Self-Esteem

Developing a good sense of self-worth can take time and effort. It will also be a journey filled with unparalleled delights, surprising turns, and an amazing finish.

The first step is to mentally get ready by ignoring your negative self-talk and stilling your inner critic. The only person in the world with the ability to quiet your inner critic is you. No one else in your life can take this step for you since the critic lives only in your thoughts.

You won't be able to achieve healthy self-esteem unless that voice isn't the main attraction. Everyone harbours an inner critic, but those who don't think well of themselves are more prone to give their critic space. Your negative self-talk restricts you in a lot of ways. It makes it harder to receive constructive criticism without losing your cool totally and makes it more difficult to perceive your failures as opportunities to grow.

Because your inner critic never stops telling you that you're not good enough to advance or get better, you are unable to change. It continuously makes comparisons between you and those you think are superior to you—people you think are funnier, smarter, more attractive, and so on.

Give it a chance, and it can come off as more convincing than your upbeat voice or the voices of others who care about and encourage you. To avoid damaging your self-esteem, you can opt to ignore or at least suppress the critical aspect of your inner voice. The next time your inner critic attempts to undermine you with doubts, recognise it. Inform that voice that although you've heard it, you don't agree with it and won't be paying attention. The first step to controlling your inner critic is to do this. Your inner critic won't go away if you just ignore it.

Making the conscious choice to react to your inner critic the next time it speaks with five verifiable, true facts about who you are is the second step to quieting it. You must deny the critic any power if you want it to stop talking. When your inner critic speaks, pay attention to the positive aspects of yourself that you are aware of. Perhaps you adore the ensemble you're sporting. Perhaps what you did was good. Prioritise those constructive thoughts over the critical one.

Ultimately, you can silence your critic by focusing on the aspects of your life that you wish to get better at. Establishing goals is the next stage in your path if you believe that you talk too much, have a negative attitude, or struggle to make friends.

How Self-Esteem Is Caused by Negative Talk

There are several reasons why people don't succeed in their endeavours. It could be the result of poor goal selection, tardiness, or a lack of preparation.

One of these reasons is poor self-esteem, and the most common way that low self-esteem arises is through negative language. Low self-esteem can also be the root cause of your inner critic or negative self-talk, which can lead to a vicious cycle. The speaker continues, "You ought to have performed better on your test." "You should have been a better friend." You have all heard them. One of the main components of your negative self-talk is the "shoulds".

Tell your inner critic to shut up if you need to shift your attention away from it. Just say "Be quiet!" You may feel more assured if you speak the words aloud. Until you sense that the negative voice is becoming less powerful, keep saying the words aloud. "BE QUIET!"

How to Define and Evaluate Your Self-Esteem

You are denying your individuality if you attempt to place a value on your life and build your self-worth based on the views of others. You're deluding yourself into thinking that being unique is unimportant. You're lying to yourself, telling yourself that you're not special, that there's no purpose for you being on Earth.

Think about your present circumstances in life. What is your great mystery exactly? What have you accomplished that nobody else on the earth could? "Hardly anything," one could argue. False! "I've never gotten an award," you could add, or "I've never made a significant contribution." These statements might be accurate, but perhaps that isn't what you want out of life. Those don't demonstrate your uniqueness as a person. You are not the world's gift to them.

The most important thing you can do to better and develop yourself is to accept that importance is relative at best and needs to be measured against society. The only person on the globe with the ability to judge your own significance is you. Killing your self-esteem is the same as letting someone else do it. The problem with personal value is that it has no agreed-upon definition.

Some people see worth in money. Some people define value in terms of possessions, kids, relationships, talent, honesty, devotion, passion, dignity, or knowledge. Everybody has a very distinct idea of what makes them valuable. Evaluating your value is like trying to calculate how much money you have on the counter at the same moment when there are pounds, euros, pesos, dollars, and yen. Which is currently more valuable to you? Which one will suit you the most for your travels? Everything depends on how you travel.

You will possess the kind of self-worth that people look up to if you can put aside other people's opinions about you. It's simple to get caught up in what other people think of you or what they think of you, but this only serves to highlight their viewpoints. You're giving other people's ideas the power to shape your choices, attitudes, routines, and—above all—your self-perception.

Have you ever made a life-changing decision solely based on what other people thought of you? It is impossible to avoid damaging your self-esteem when you act in this way. You suffer when your need for approval from others is too great.

To find out whether the things you believe about yourself are true or if you have just gradually come to believe them based on the opinions of others, you need to evaluate your sense of self-worth. It's possible that they convinced you of your opinions, and you never bothered to challenge them. If you have an unfounded belief, you need to know what it is and how you got to believe it before you can modify it. After that, you can attempt to unlearn it by challenging it. Make a list of these problems and make an effort to accept the reality of the circumstance.

Think about the following hypothetical situation:

Monnie has always loved to dance, but she no longer does it in public. She told her best friend Winnie one day how much she enjoyed dancing. People made fun of Monnie for being overweight. When Winnie told her other mutual friends about Monnie's love of dancing, they remarked that someone with Monnie's weight would never be good at it. Monnie eventually ceased dancing, even while she was by herself, after coming to believe them.

When her mother saw, she inquired as to why Monnie had stopped dancing. She eventually opened up on what her friends had said about her and how it had affected her after much convincing.

This is a great example of how other people's opinions may warp your own self-perception. You have no control over the past or your emotions at any given moment, but you do have control over the things that shape your thoughts, feelings, and behaviour going forward. You have the option of wings or shackles. The key to having a strong sense of self-worth is knowing that you can choose what is important to you.

Setting the Need for Mental and Physical Health First The journey begins with the realisation that our bodily and emotional well-being are our most precious possessions. We discuss how important it is to put self-care first when pursuing wealth building in the first segment. By realising that the foundation of long-term success is a sound body and mind, we create the conditions for an abundant life in every way. We learn from anecdotes that highlight the transforming potential of holistic health that financial success is not an afterthought but rather a prerequisite for maintaining one's well-being.

Three Steps to Putting Your Physical and Mental Health First for Overall Success First Step: Declare Health a Top Priority

Start by realising how important your physical and emotional well-being are to your total achievement. Realise that your health is the cornerstone around which all of your endeavours are constructed. Recognise that a healthy body and mind establish the best circumstances for long-term success, paving the way for both current and future riches.

Step 2: Include Techniques for Self-Care

Examine the necessity of incorporating self-care routines into your everyday schedule. Accept practices that improve your physical and mental well-being, such as regular exercise, meditation, a balanced diet, and enough sleep.

Make time for rest and renewal a priority, understanding that these activities enhance your general health. Including self-care into your daily routine will improve your ability to pursue financial objectives with vigour and resilience.

Section 8

Step 3: Get Ideas from Storytelling That Transforms Take inspiration from true stories that demonstrate how holistic health can change lives. Learn from those who prioritised their well-being and attained financial success. Recognise that maintaining your well-being is essential to achieving prosperity and not a luxury.

You may create a balanced and fulfilling life where success is determined not just by outward achievements but also by the inner peace that arises from a healthy body and mind by incorporating health into your goal of wealth creation.

CHAPTER 8 8.2: Stress Reduction and Mindfulness

As we go more, we uncover the practice of stress management and mindfulness, two vital life skills. In the second part, we explore the technique of developing present-moment awareness, which enables us to face difficulties head-on and remain composed. Learning stress-reduction strategies gives us the fortitude to face challenges head-on without compromising our health.

We discover via stories that highlight the benefits of mindfulness that preserving our ability to manage stress and keep our composure is essential to preserving both our personal and professional well-being.

Three Easy Steps to Become an Expert in Stress Management and Mindfulness
Step 1: Accept Awareness of the Present

Start by adopting the mindfulness technique, commonly referred to as present-moment awareness. Set aside time every day to practise mindfulness, whether it is through deep breathing, meditation, or just taking in your environment. By practicing this, you can avoid becoming overwhelmed by stress and improve your capacity to respond to obstacles with calmness and clarity.

Step 2: Acquire Stress Reduction Skills
Investigate the world of stress-reduction strategies that appeal to you. These can be journaling, gradual muscular relaxation, deep breathing techniques,

or taking up enjoyable hobbies. Gaining the ability to handle difficulties without sacrificing your mental and emotional health comes from mastering these strategies.

Acknowledge that stress management is a talent that supports both career and personal development.

Create a solid network of social support.

Create a network of contacts that you can rely on when you need them. When others are in need, assist them as well. Keep your friends and family near by. Possessing a solid support network increases confidence by fostering a sense of security.

To improve your self-esteem, go to workshops or therapy.

Attend workshops on raising self-esteem whenever you can because the experts can offer you insightful advice, coping mechanisms, and self-esteem-boosting methods.

Reward yourself when you reach your objectives.

Celebrate your accomplishments whenever you reach a goal, no matter how modest. Your confidence will grow and your sense of value will be reinforced. One of the main components of increasing self-esteem and bravery to pursue greater achievements is having a sense of accomplishments.

Develop compassion and understanding for oneself.

Treat yourself with the same compassion and understanding that you would others. Acknowledge your thoughts, feelings, and flaws without passing judgement on yourself. This aids in changing the conversation from negative to positive aspects of you.

Be willing to adapt and evolve as a person.

Changes present many opportunities for personal development and are a normal aspect of life. Always approach new situations, obstacles, and educational opportunities with a growth mentality. It enables you to adapt to different circumstances and overcome obstacles.

Let go of the rest and concentrate on what you can manage.

There are many things that we can control and many things that are out of our hands. Stress and negativity are brought on by concentrating on things that are out of our control. On the other hand, concentrating on the things that we can control, such as our thoughts, deeds, and reactions, gives you the ability to make wiser and more beneficial judgements.

Take pauses to recover and avoid becoming burned out.

To rejuvenate yourself, take short pauses from whatever you are doing on a regular basis. This will lessen fatigue and stress on the body and mind. This helps you perceive issues or obstacles from several angles and improves your capacity to finish tasks or activities.

Accept challenges as chances for personal development

Difficulties present chances to grow, develop resilience, and discover your inner strength. Consequently, embrace difficulties and difficult circumstances wholeheartedly as they are not obstacles to overcome. In actuality, they are stepping stones towards personal development.

Discard stereotypes and celebrate variety

Stereotype refers to oversimplified, preconceived notions, ideas, and presumptions about individuals, objects, or anything else. This phenomenon is undesirable in general because it disregards the diversity of objects or persons. Discrimination and biassed judgements may result from this. Since every person or circumstance is different and requires a new perspective, it is crucial to question stereotypes. Your self-confidence and personal development will benefit from this.

When you feel self-conscious, try practicing self-compassion.

When you doubt your skills or your personality, try not to criticise yourself and instead, act with self-compassion.

Treat yourself with the same compassion that you would show others in times of need.

Dispute the notion that you require approval from others.

Recognise that you don't require confirmation of your deservingness or an outside viewpoint. Have faith in your accomplishments and principles, and embrace who you are. Even if you can grow from criticism or unfavourable comments, they are unable to determine your actual value.

How Much Self-Compassion Do I Have?

An essential element of mental health and wellbeing is self-compassion. It entails being compassionate, understanding, and accepting of ourselves despite our struggles and setbacks. Studies have indicated that practicing self-compassion can result in reduced levels of anxiety and depression, enhanced resilience, and elevated life satisfaction. However, how can self-compassion be quantified? How can we determine whether we're getting better at this crucial skill?

I use multiple methods to assess my degree of self-compassion, such as reviewing my journal entries on a regular basis and asking close friends for their opinions. I consider how I am doing and how self-compassionate I have been in handling my accomplishments and setbacks as I go over my journals. I can detect if I am being too hard on myself or too gentle on myself by looking back at my failures, successes, and reactions to them. This can have a big influence on my life. I can also see places where I need to work on forgiveness, mindfulness, or good self-talk by reading my notebooks.

Asking friends for their honest opinions is another useful strategy I use to evaluate my level of self-compassion. I might say harsh judgements of myself or engage in negative self-talk whether out for a walk or having a chat. My buddies provide me an other viewpoint at these times. They inspire me to treat myself with more kindness and serve as a reminder of the good things that have happened to me. Their encouragement enables me to see that I am not the only one going through difficult times and that I can always improve.

You will have a greater understanding of additional techniques and approaches for measuring self-compassion by the end of this chapter. Given how closely related self-esteem and self-compassion are, don't be afraid to read Chapter 3 again.

How to Assess Your Level of Self-Compassion

The act of treating oneself with love, consideration, and understanding when facing challenges, setbacks, and suffering is known as self-compassion. You can assess your degree of self-compassion in the following ways:

● Examine your inner monologue: Take note of the things you say to yourself when something goes wrong. Are you empathetic and kind, or do you speak in a harsh or judgmental manner? Try to think about yourself in a more compassionate way if you find that you have a propensity to be critical of yourself. To find trends, try keeping a notebook and documenting these occurrences. Where is it simplest to treat oneself with kindness? Where do you treat yourself the worst?

Examine your practices for self-care: Are your emotional and physical needs being met? Do you schedule time for activities that relax and make you happy? Making self-care a priority is a self-kindness practice.

Take the "Best Friend" quiz: Take a moment to consider your priorities, actions, and words towards yourself. Would you tell your best friend to talk to oneself and treat themselves this way if they were in the same situation? It's time to reassess such beliefs and actions if you would feel upset if your friend hurt themself!

● Think about how you handle mistakes and failures: do you punish yourself and brood over them, or do you accept them and move on in a compassionate manner? Accepting our flaws and errors as a necessary component of being human is a key component of self-compassion.

● Consider your principles and objectives: Are your expectations of yourself reasonable? Are you aiming to achieve objectives that complement your moral principles and give your life purpose? Setting difficult but attainable goals and rewarding yourself for your progress rather than your perfection are two aspects of practicing self-compassion.

Keep in mind that practicing self-compassion requires patience and work. You can begin to develop a more loving and compassionate relationship with yourself by being aware of your thoughts, behaviours, and interactions.

Scales of Self-Compassion

In order to gauge your level of self-compassion, there are several tests and scales available. These are a handful that are widely acknowledged in the field of psychological study.

Scale of Self-Compassion (SCS): A pioneering researcher in the field of self-compassion, Kristin Neff created the 26-item Self-Compassion Scale (SCS). Six dimensions of self-compassion are measured by the scale: over-identification, mindfulness, self-judgment, self-kindness, isolation, and shared humanity. A scale of agreement or disagreement is applied to statements such as "I'm kind to myself when I'm experiencing suffering" and "I'm intolerant and impatient towards those aspects of my personality I don't like."

Neff Self-Compassion Scale (NSCS): Kristin Neff created this additional 26-item assessment. While it measures the same six aspects of self-compassion as the SCS, its design aims to be more inclusive and culturally sensitive. On the scale, participants are asked to indicate how much they agree or disagree with phrases such as "I try to be understanding and patient towards aspects of my personality I don't like" and "I'm tolerant of my own flaws and inadequacies."

Fierce Self-Compassion Scale (FSCS): Developed by Kristin Neff and coauthor Christopher Germer, the FSCS consists of 21 items. Along with other related conceptions like self-criticism, self-reassurance, and self-acceptance, it evaluates self-compassion. Respondents score how much they agree or disagree with statements such as "I accept my flaws and shortcomings without judgement" and "When I fail at something, I remind myself that I'm only human."

These measures can be helpful in determining areas for improvement and evaluating one's degree of self-compassion. It's crucial to keep in mind, though, that self-compassion is a complicated, multidimensional concept that cannot be adequately described by a single survey.

Chapter 6: Cultivating Self-Respect

Merely being conscious of the aspects of oneself that you wish to modify is insufficient. You need to adopt a change-oriented mindset before you can start boosting your self-esteem and loving yourself, as well as your confidence. People are afraid of change a lot. The human mind is inherently consistent, particularly due to its propensity to mechanise specific actions and cognitive functions. You will learn how to cultivate a mindset in this chapter that will enable you to be prepared for the good things that are going to happen in your life. It is more probable that you will succeed if you have perspective about what to expect and the obstacles in your path.

Getting Rid of the Instant Gratification Trap

Even if it wasn't your indulgence day, have you ever failed at a diet? It is not unusual for people to turn to their favourite foods for comfort when they are feeling down. Nevertheless, they are not very successful in sticking to their diet thanks to this quick satisfaction. People demand results right now, which is the issue with quick gratification. It is much easier to give in and indulge in an additional dessert or visit their favourite fast food restaurant than it is to wait to feel better by digesting their feelings.

One important factor in rapid gratification is social networking. People exchange ideas and pictures with the hopes of becoming somewhat well-known among their followers. Some people go further than others with this, developing an obsession with their social media presence and getting likes. Setting and achieving objectives in the real world seems insignificant in a world where social media makes it simple to look for fast results.

Willpower and the Marshmallow Experiment

A well-known experiment on rapid gratification was conducted in the 1960s and 1970s at Stanford University by psychologist Walter Mischel. The exam established the foundation for a large portion of the current research on self-control, which has been strongly associated with success. In the study, Mischel and his colleagues used marshmallows to test a group of preschoolers' self-control exercises. A researcher took the child to a room. If the researcher decided to leave the room, they were informed. The scientist would come back right away and offer the child a marshmallow if they rang a bell at any time. Young children who patiently awaited the researcher's return to get their reward would be given an additional marshmallow.

In the first phase of the marshmallow experiment, some preschoolers rang the bell, while others had to wait for the second marshmallow. The results were inconsistent. The experiment's follow-up, however, was unmixed. After talking with their parents, Mischel and his research team reanalyzed these children as teenagers. Preschoolers who demonstrated the ability to resist impulses and wait for the marshmallow on the SAT scored higher overall. Furthermore, their parents were more likely to say that they were capable of managing stress, organising, exercising self-control, and using logic.

This study concludes that if you want to succeed in life, you need to break free from the trap of instant pleasure. More recently, Mischel became more demanding when working with psychologists Yuichi Shoda of the University of Washington and B.J. Casey of the Weill Cornell Medical Centre. They ran a laboratory test that is frequently used to assess an adult's self-control in order to locate 59 of the youngsters who had taken part in the marshmallow experiment with the assistance of colleagues. The findings demonstrated that, even though the initial trial was conducted over forty years ago, most people's preschool-based self-control persisted throughout their lives. On the self-control test, those who had been able to withstand the urge and earn a second marshmallow performed better.

The Dual-Temperature Impulse System

Further research on the subject and an examination of brain imaging during an MRI test to assess self-control revealed differences in the brains of those who had higher self-control compared to those who do not. These matched the findings of Mischel's initial tests, which he clarified using a "hot-and-cool" paradigm. In other words, willpower breaks down when the emotional and impulsive hot system takes precedence over the rational cool system. It is action-based, leading to the consumption of the marshmallow without thinking through the long-term effects. In contrast, the cool system is a cognitive system that enables you to consider the implications. It enables you to think about your objectives and the ways in which your deeds, emotions, and experiences contribute to achieving them. It seems a bit like the devil and an angel are considering your alternatives while perched on your shoulder.

The comprehension of the interindividual variations in the hot-and-cold system is an incomplete aspect of this research. It is evident that an individual's ability to control their impulses is a lifelong trait, but the variables that influence an individual's willpower are still unknown. Does that imply that someone who lacks willpower will never accomplish their objectives? Not always.

10. Lead by Example

Just as it's usual for kids to copy their parents' thoughts and behaviours, families should ideally create a positive example for their kids to follow in order for them to develop a growth mindset. Therefore, make every effort to model a growth mindset for your kids, and when you fail to do so, attempt to recognise and correct your own behaviour.

If you frequently say negative things, consider substituting them with statements that are more focused on personal development, like "I'm not good at this at all" or "This is very difficult."

For instance, "I'm not as good as I want, I have to practise more," as well as "I haven't learned it yet, I need a lot of effort, but I know it's worth it in the end."

Additionally, when something doesn't work out the way you had hoped, try stating something like, "I didn't do well this time, but I can't wait to learn a lot from the process and try again," rather than, "I ruined it completely."

under a perfect world, kids would learn that even under difficult circumstances, they should always look for chances to exhibit good attitudes and adopt a "half-glass" viewpoint. You teach your kids that there is always a bright side to each obstacle or error by acting in this way.

This chapter demonstrates how developing unwavering confidence and a robust, healthy sense of self-worth are the cornerstones of a successful life. Even if you may have had a difficult upbringing and unfavourable events that weakened your self-esteem as a child and adolescent, those things don't have to keep you back any more. You might finally find your strength today and start living the life you've always wanted. It's not required of you to stay the same. It's not necessary for you to cling to the lifestyle that brought you pain. Let the brightness of unwavering confidence shine into your life today. Cast your eyes towards the horizon and begin to imagine a better dream. You are capable of having a strong sense of faith and self-worth, and you will. Chapters two through seven walk you through the six steps to developing extraordinary confidence that can change your life. Let's plunge into the next chapter, where you will first take the time to understand who you are and who you want to become, and begin this path to a life of freedom and amazing adventures. You're all set to enter your realm of boundless triumphs.

Discovering Yourself

Have you ever considered your identity in the absence of the experiences you encountered? People's personalities are greatly influenced by the locations they visit, the people they meet, the circumstances they grow up in, and the surroundings they are in. These things have an impact on the ideas, values, routines, and objectives you adopt and live by. Finding your true self can be one of life's most rewarding journeys. However, if you think you already know who you are and that there is nothing more to learn about yourself, then self-discovery may also seem like a route not worth following.

Refusing to take advantage of the chance to learn more about who you are runs the risk of causing you to spend the rest of your life living with self-perceptions that impede you from reaching your greatest potential. Adolescents who take seriously the quest to find their own identity and value at a young age, before reaching adulthood, end up becoming very successful and well-rounded people. Individuals who put off taking this important step towards realising who they truly are run the risk of living years in denial and accepting a life that is unworthy of them. The worst thing about this tragedy is that by the time you begin to realise who you are again, it's usually too late and old age is drawing near. You can't go back in time and accomplish all that you could have in your adolescence and early adulthood.

I hope you avoid this destiny and regret not taking the time and making the effort to find your true self. This chapter will assist you in considering who you are even if you are still a teenager with your whole life ahead of you. You will learn how to ask the proper questions in this chapter, which will lead to the answers. You are more complex than what you perceive yourself to be. Are you prepared to allow yourself to see aspects of who you are that you may not have previously given much thought to? Are you prepared to examine everything that makes you who you are and to unpack your entire being?

The fact that your ideas do not have to define who you are is one of the most important, profound, and transformative insights about your true identity that you will ever learn! Have you ever noticed how readily your daily thoughts may shape your perception of who you think you are? Let's say you are perpetually trapped in a mental cycle where you believe you lack skill, beauty, competence, and the ability to accomplish your goals. In that circumstance, you can easily begin to accept the teachings included in those ideas as true and real. It is still necessary for the notions your thoughts are planting about you to hold true, even though you have chosen to believe them. The fact that most individuals don't challenge their beliefs and distance themselves from them is what causes them to get so wedded to what they believe those thoughts to be about them. Many people accept negative thoughts as part of who they are when they surface and convey depressing information to their conscious and subconscious minds, failing to recognise that thoughts are just suggestions that may or may not be real. Your ideas can only arouse sensations and emotions in you that are consistent with the statements they are expressing if you acknowledge them as true. You may consider, for instance, "Did you notice how everyone stared at you when you first walked into the room, and nobody even bothered to say hello or smile? That is a dead giveaway that you are boring and unlikable to everyone.

You may feel a range of feelings following this thinking, including discomfort, sadness, hopelessness, anger, rejection, irritation, insecurity, and a general feeling of being downtrodden and depressed. It would be easy to assume that you are a pessimistic, miserable, unlovable, and ugly person if you frequently experience the same thoughts, sensations, and unpleasant emotions. This will then motivate you to connect with those internal sentiments and ideas. This implies that you will also begin to reinforce the notion that you are uninteresting and unlikable. This conviction will start to mould your thinking, affect your choices and the things you do because it has a place in your heart. Because you think no one likes you and you're not pretty enough, you isolate yourself and put up walls around yourself. It's also possible to start being antisocial and rude to other people, which will make it difficult for them to become friends. You resist compliments and pleasant things and find it hard to believe anything positive that is said.

Chapter 10: Complete Hell Yeses

The entire meeting is defined by first and last impressions. Try this with those you encounter during the workweek, such as bellhops, newsstand vendors, and employees at coffee shops. Ask them about their day while grinning. Grin and leave them with a kind word for the day. Return the following day and follow suit.

You'll notice that they'll greet you more easily, primarily because you demonstrated to them what a confident, well-mannered, and cultured person you are, but also because they remembered you. Informing the other person how much you enjoyed your interaction will give them more self-confidence and help them recall your interaction as a positive one in later social situations.

One of the best ways to demonstrate to others that you are confident enough to see their qualities is to acknowledge them. People around you may be expressing their problems with you as well, so you should give them the freedom to express themselves. You will grow as a person as a result, since leaders understand the value of win-win strategies and mindsets. People will appreciate you more if you acknowledge their successes and difficulties. It will make your interactions more human.

In your arguments, make use of facts. Chit talks should be reserved for strangers rather than for those you need to influence. Understand the topic of the discussion and do some fact-finding. If you presented all of your facts clearly and concisely, even if you lose a debate, it will still be a minor triumph. The other team will be aware of what they are up against and that you fight back before losing.

When communicating, use humour. Comedy is a fantastic way to break the ice and can help with a lot of awkward social situations. Because they portray you as a self-assured individual who isn't hesitant to point out their own shortcomings, jokes that make fun of you are frequently the funniest. If your supervisor decides to call you out on your errors or failures, there isn't a joke witty enough to get you out of his or her office. Therefore, avoid using comedy as a diversion from important business conversations. If the circumstance permits, by all means crack a joke, but take care not to come across as unprofessional.

Engage in conversation with others. The best treatment for social anxiety or shyness is practice. Throughout the day, strike up a conversation with at least five strangers to flex your social skills and feel comfortable interacting with a wide spectrum of people. In this manner, you acquire experience and develop your ability to react to a variety of stimuli, enabling you to recognise the essential people's conversational style and aptitude when they approach you.

Unwind. Discover some relaxation techniques and give them a try. You might need to try a few before you find the one that truly helps you deal with your anxiety. Not all of them will be effective. You will need to develop the ability to maintain composure; else, you can find it difficult to regulate how you react in crucial circumstances. Slamming doors, losing your temper, or yelling will only make you appear more insecure. Because you are choosing to flee the problem rather than remain composed and work through it, others will perceive you as a young and insecure person.

Keep your enthusiasm in check. We can frequently overwhelm and exhaust our audience when we are confident in ourselves. To make our point, we begin to speak louder, faster, and with a lot of gestures. Reduce the intensity of your motions to your waist, slow down between points, and halt. In this manner, you'll come out as more composed and assured in your presentation. Speaking quickly could give the impression to your opponent that you are hurrying to get to the point quickly rather than making a compelling or interesting enough argument.

Setting Up Healthful Limits

Setting up healthy boundaries is one of the most important and transformational steps in the process of freeing oneself from the grip of codependency. Codependents frequently struggle with ambiguous or nonexistent boundaries, which can make it difficult for them to uphold their sense of self and create healthy, fulfilling relationships. This chapter explores the critical role that boundaries play in codependency recovery and provides helpful, doable actions to help you set and maintain boundaries.

The Role of Limitations in the Healing Process

Boundaries are the mental and physical lines that you draw to protect your health and draw a boundary between your identity and that of others. They provide as the foundation for navigating the complexities of your interactions and relationships. Boundaries are essential to the codependency recovery process because they help you rebuild your identity and create stronger, longer-lasting relationships. The following are the main purposes that boundaries serve:

1. Self-Definition: Setting boundaries is essential to defining your identity and creating a self that exists apart from other people. This fundamental procedure is essential for breaking free from codependent behaviours since it makes it possible to acknowledge your own worth and values.

2. Protection of Emotional Well-Being: Sound boundaries serve as bulwarks, defending your emotional integrity. They serve as a barrier against the overwhelming impact of other people's feelings and behaviours, which is a frequent problem in codependent relationships.

3. Facilitation of Self-Respect: You can communicate self-respect by setting and maintaining boundaries. Others will then

be more inclined to appreciate you and your needs as a result.

4. Empowerment of Autonomy: Having boundaries gives you the ability to stay independent and autonomous. You are not unduly influenced by other people, so you may follow your own interests, come to your own conclusions, and strive towards your own goals.

5. Resentment Mitigation: Unmet needs and unspoken boundaries sometimes lead codependents to harbour resentment. Establishing and communicating clear boundaries significantly reduces the likelihood of animosity developing in your relationships.

6. Healthy Dynamics Cultivation: Having boundaries helps create more positive dynamics in relationships. They promote open, sincere communication, respect for one another, and recognition of the needs and preferences of all parties concerned.

Concrete Procedures for Defining Boundaries

Healthy boundary setting and maintenance are essential components of codependency recovery. The subsequent actions are useful strategies to help you create and keep efficient boundaries:

1. Self-reflection is the first step in the process of introspection. Think about your existing boundaries and where they may be insufficient or unhealthy. Review previous situations where you felt your limits were violated or where you weren't sure how far your boundaries extended.

2. Acknowledgment of Your Requirements: Acquire a thorough comprehension of your requirements and preferences in all areas of your life, including social, professional, and personal connections. Establishing limits starts with understanding your own needs.

3. Effective Communication: Setting boundaries requires effective communication at all times. Set limits in a straightforward, aggressive, and non-aggressive manner. Use "I" words to express your feelings and wants. For example, "I need time alone in the evenings to relax."

4. Why Consistency Matters: Maintaining boundaries requires consistency. Maintaining your limits at all times is crucial, even if it is difficult or painful to do so.

5. Self-Care is Crucial: Make self-care a top priority as a way to support and maintain your limits. Self-care, which includes your mental, emotional, and physical health, is evidence of your limits.

6. Accept the Power of "No": Being able to say "no" when necessary is one of the most important abilities in the field of creating boundaries. It is crucial to understand that saying no to a request or opportunity does not mean that you

are disregarding the person; rather, it is just a statement of your boundaries and needs.

7. Seek Advice: Consult a therapist, family member, or trusted friend about your boundary-setting attempts. Their assistance, inspiration, and direction can be quite helpful while you focus on this crucial part of your rehabilitation.

8. Adapt to Diverse partnerships: Acknowledge that different partnerships may have shifting boundaries. It's possible that what is OK for a close friend and not appropriate for a coworker or family member. Adjust your limits based on the particulars of each relationship.

9. Define Consequences: It's critical to outline what will happen if your limits are crossed. Make it plain to others what will happen if they cross your boundaries, and be ready to enforce them if needed.

Spend some time in the company of nature.

Take a stroll. Maintain a strong relationship with nature. You are not need to visit a forest or the seashore. Simply head to the closest park to take in the picturesque scenery in your area.

Spend a minute or thirty seconds massaging your palms together.

The act of rubbing your palms together produces friction and warmth. This lifts your spirits and deflects bad vibes.

Avoid being negative.

Keep your distance from negative people and surround yourself with positive, happy, and hopeful people.

Set a firm boundary.

People need to know exactly what you will and won't put up with. This keeps you in charge of your life overall and your energies. It is your responsibility to teach others how to treat you.

Reacting negatively to others is not appropriate.

Positive responses can defuse negative people. Saying "thank you for your opinion" while grinning will let you get away from someone who is demeaning you.

Don't give the beast any more food.

Determine to keep your positive attitude even in the face of adversity. Detachment practice is the best method to do this.

When you're feeling down, close your eyes and recall pleasant times. Consider your objectives. Consider everything for which you are thankful.

If you continue to surround yourself with positive thoughts, negativity will have no place in your life.

Imagine a bubble.

Shut your eyes and concentrate on your breathing each morning. Shut off any distracting thoughts and focus just on the ups and downs of your chest with each inhalation.

Pay attention to your breathing. Eliminate any distracting ideas that come to mind.

Consider yourself to be in a holy bubble right now. Positive energy envelops you as this energetic bubble replenishes your energetic field. You can shut off bad energy by using this bubble.

Even in really stressful situations or when someone else is freaking out, this bubble helps you stay composed.

Engage in an aerobic workout.

Running, walking, dancing, swimming, and cycling are examples of aerobic exercises that help you burn off extra energy. It supports your sense of grounding and helps you repel negative energy and feelings.

Finally, resolve to choose a good outlook every day. Live a happy and thankful life.

Always make the decision to see the positive side of things.

Positive Psychology in Chapter 7

The field of positive psychology emerged in the United States during the 1960s and 1970s. In order to make psychological principles more accessible to laypeople who may not be well-versed in psychological theory, positive psychology, or PP, began as a movement that tried to apply psychological principles to daily situations. Instead of only attempting to enable people to exist and survive, positive psychology focuses on allowing them to flourish in their life. Can you perceive the distinction? There is a process that will help us live longer when we are just trying to survive, and the desire to live is something we all possess. However, in order for humanity to fully thrive, some requirements must be satisfied.

The distinction between thriving and existing is this. Your life may appear one way while you are only trying to survive. You might be taking care of your basic requirements as an individual, which include having a place to sleep, food to eat, a job, and other necessities for survival. On the other hand, you will encounter a more profound aspect of life on Earth when you are thriving. A flourishing individual has a wealth of life experiences. Deeply painful experiences can be integrated with deeply joyful and happy experiences by them. A person who is thriving will be able to establish relationships with the others they wish to interact with. They'll be getting close to reaching their full potential as people. They will also be able to assist others in obtaining the necessary resources to develop into fully realised versions of themselves. There are several sources of this flourishing. These consist of meaning, relationships, self-expression, and connection. One major one is meaningfulness.

People look for purpose in life throughout their entire lives. We may not always be able to locate and perceive meaningfulness. It's something we frequently have to strive towards. Certain circumstances surround each person from birth; some are born into poverty, some into the middle class, and yet others into the upper classes of society. Even though their lives may be easier for those at the top, everyone must find purpose in their lives.

Meaning is something we have to define for ourselves; it can come from the smallest things or the biggest events in our life. The goal of positive psychology is to help us discover purpose in life so that we can grow and thrive.

Another essential component of flourishing is self-expression. People who never express themselves will discover that they are lacking a vital component of human functioning. To accomplish this correctly, people need to learn how to express themselves without passing judgement. Another thing that is necessary for humans to flourish is connection. Most people need to learn how to connect with others in order to thrive. Since we are all descended from another person, it is necessary for us to relate to others on this fundamental level. Humans cannot survive if we do not grow up under the care of other humans. At this point, a connection is so much needed. To discover our position in the world, we have to learn early on how to be connected to our family or, at the very least, understand what family means to us. Human life is not human existence without connection.

We can pursue these life goals with the framework provided by positive psychology. Learning how to obtain these things that we so sorely need can be done through positive psychology. Among the strategies for achieving these goals is optimistic thinking.

Your confidence and sense of calmness in all that you do can be greatly enhanced by positive thinking. Thinking positively helps you view the world more clearly, deal with challenging people more effectively, go through the grieving process more easily, and generally lead a healthy, happy life. Although everyone approaches positive thinking differently, there is one thing that is certain. It is essential to our daily existence. As was previously established, our bodies have a profound and intimate relationship with our thoughts, and our thoughts and emotions have a significant impact on our bodies. Recall that your thoughts define you.

Negative thinking, on the other hand, sets you up to become what you detest, to fall short of your own standards, and to cease thinking and acting in a healthy way. Consistently thinking negatively causes you to belittle both other people and yourself. As a result, you keep having negative thoughts and expectations, which feeds the cycle. Physical signs of it include tense muscles, stress, and even compromised immunological function. Furthermore, negative thinking is, to some extent, a kind of self-loathing. You have negative self-perceptions, which you act out of, in a sense, to support. You may just give up on attempting to change the way you look or carry yourself in public if you don't think you are attractive or handsome. You begin to see yourself as the most flawed version of yourself.

Having said that, negative thoughts must be managed, if not completely eradicated. Furthermore, it impacts not just your health but also the people in your immediate vicinity, your career, and how others see you. In the end, having pessimistic thoughts keeps you from having fun in life. To enhance your general attitude towards the community you live in, as well as your mood, mental and physical well-being, you must learn to think positively.

It all begins with a shift of viewpoint. You need to reflect on yourself. What aspects of yourself do I find lacking? Why do I find fault with myself? You must first recognise the ways in which you denigrate yourself. Some people might find this method simpler than others. Some people struggle with their bodies. Body dysmorphic disorder is a condition where a person feels constantly self-critical of their appearance or that they are constantly making negative assumptions about it, both of themselves and maybe other people. A person like this will have to pick up two new skills. The first step is to determine what they genuinely want and can accomplish to improve their appearance. This could be taking up running as a habit or another type of physical activity. It might entail eating healthier. It just needs to be something mild and doable, whatever comes down. Letting rid of whatever negative thoughts you may have about your looks is the second challenge. You may just brush that off and say something like, "I've been working out lately, so that's something I can do to look better." "I can handle this area alone with that much work," you say, forgiving the remainder. That voice, which is essentially saying that you look awful and horrible, is something you have to confront because it is you. Bullies and abusive persons might occasionally be a part of our lives, telling us hurtful things about ourselves. However, it usually originates from our own awareness.

Thinking positively indicates that you are beginning to recognise the lovely things that you do encounter on a regular basis and are moving away from the viewpoint of doom and despair. Not because we don't have any wonderful experiences in our lives, but rather because we aren't taking advantage of the ones that are directly in front of us. It's not all sunshine and rainbows, as you can see. Positive thinking is changing your perspective just a little bit, from "Ugh, it's dark outside today, and I don't want to go to work" to "It is dark outside today, but I am going to do my best at work and maybe take a nap afterward." Thinking positively should be achievable and reasonable.

It is crucial to address motivation, particularly in those who are depressed. Motivation is one of the main factors influencing depression. Depression is mostly caused by a lack of motivation, which frequently spirals into a vicious cycle of unhappiness and hopelessness. Although motivation is a difficult word to define, we can pretty well say with confidence that those who are in better physical health tend to be more driven. Your motivation will wain if you devote all of your time to addiction or bad behaviours, as this will perpetuate the cycle. It is regrettable, but this does occur.

High Emotional Intelligence Example

Since each person has a unique personality, there are differences in the ways that different people acquire their intellect. Here are some typical behaviours of highly intelligent persons in regulated settings, such as the workplace:

They are able to express themselves freely and respectfully without worrying that they will offend someone. They also frequently demonstrate resilience in the face of new initiatives, even when they disagree with them. They are also always adaptable. They enjoy socialising with their coworkers outside of work hours. They are free to be creative, and that is celebrated. They frequently participate actively in meetings and offer their opinions when they have them.

Leadership is one of the most significant areas where having a strong emotional intelligence is beneficial. A team that is more unified and committed to a single goal can be assembled by leaders with high emotional intelligence (EI). Rather than only producing to get things done, they frequently have a greater sense of passion for the task they accomplish. In addition to inspiring and empowering staff, a leader with a high emotional intelligence (EI) is adept at making difficult and complex decisions while demonstrating a strong emotional response.

Being emotionally intelligent does not equate to being content or upbeat all the time. It merely indicates that the individual can make wise choices about what to do in challenging circumstances. They are able to control their emotions such that they don't influence the decisions they make.

Low Emotional Intelligence Examples

Low emotional intelligence has a big impact on how we interact with other people, just as high emotional intelligence is highly valued in both professional and everyday settings. Many social interactions become unpleasant and challenging when people with poor emotional intelligence, such as friends, family, employers, and coworkers, are involved. Most of the time, it might be an issue with your own emotional intelligence.

Here are nine typical symptoms to assist you determine whether you have low emotional intelligence or not:

arguing with one another all the time.

Most people have certainly encountered at least one person in their lives who constantly seems to be picking fights with other people. You will have arguments with these kinds of people from time to time with friends, family, and occasionally even complete strangers. This is because persons with low emotional intelligence find it difficult to read the feelings of others and to debate with them without taking it into account.

incapacity to comprehend how others are feeling.

People with low emotional intelligence (EI) frequently have a very poor awareness of the emotions and feelings of others. For example, they find it difficult to comprehend why their coworkers are irritated with them or why their friends could be upset with them. Furthermore, they frequently feel that they need to be the ones irritated with other people due to the expectations placed on them by others to comprehend their emotions. Although this is true for persons with high EI, people with low EI are unable to accurately gauge how others are feeling. People with little emotional intelligence sometimes become extremely irritated just by talking about feelings.

believing that people are excessively sensitive in general.

Joking around at inappropriate times is a trait of those with inadequate emotional intelligence. For instance, people might jest immediately following a traumatic incident or burial. A person with poor emotional intelligence (EI) could think that others are being overly sensitive when they don't get the expected response to their inappropriate jokes. They find it difficult to empathise with others, which makes it difficult for them to gauge the emotional climate in some circumstances.

not being open to hearing other people out.

Individuals with poor emotional intelligence (EI) frequently believe they are always correct, fiercely maintain their position, and are unreceptive to criticism. These folks are usually quite judgmental of other people's emotions and pessimistic.

laying blame on others for mishaps.

Individuals lacking in emotional intelligence are often not aware of how their own emotions might cause issues and are not adept at managing them. Their first instinct when something doesn't go their way is to point the finger at others around them. They frequently place the blame on the circumstances or the actions of others. These people frequently refute their actions by claiming that they had no other option and that others are the ones who are insensitive to their predicament. They often claim victimhood as a way to escape accountability.

unable to deal with circumstances that are emotionally charged.

People with low EI have trouble understanding strong emotions when the situation calls for them. To avoid having to cope with confrontations, they usually want to get away from these circumstances. These people also frequently keep their sentiments and emotions hidden from other people.

Unexpected Outbursts of Emotion.

One of the key components of high emotional intelligence is the capacity to control and manage one's emotions, as we discovered from studying the cases of such individuals. It might be difficult for people who lack emotional intelligence to recognise and control their emotions. Unexpected and seemingly uncontrollable emotional outbursts are common in them.

It's hard to keep friendships going.

People with low EI find it difficult to form bonds and form friendships with others since they come across as harsh and insensitive a lot of the time. Those with low EI find it difficult to maintain friendships because it takes mutual give and take. They also struggle with other aspects of friendship that call for compassion, emotional support, and sharing of feelings.

Lack of empathy.

People with poor emotional intelligence (EI) frequently struggle to empathise with others because they have difficulty identifying the feelings of others. It is extremely difficult for them to see things from the other person's perspective, let alone empathise, because they just do not grasp the emotions that the other person is experiencing.

Become a behavioural profiler or internet detective.

You will strengthen your case even more if you have the chance to learn beforehand who you will be meeting and some background information about them. After that, you'll be ready to ask pertinent questions of the people you meet. If not, practise behavioural profiling with the readily available visual cues (recall Sherlock Holmes, who could infer a person's vocation only by observing their hands).

Never assume that others will concur with you.

According to research, a large number of us are guilty of "assumed similarity bias." It is illogical to assume that someone you are speaking with shares your opposition to a particular political party. Fun discourse will come from debates. However, you're likely to start off incorrectly and wind up in your mouth if you think that everyone thinks the same way you do.

Aim to gain knowledge from every encounter you have with a new person.

There's a chance that someone you've never met before was placed and experienced things you haven't. People from different regions, such as different countries, will provide you with fresh perspectives. They won't open until you express interest in them. Your understanding of foreign nations, cultures, and languages will grow, and you'll eventually become a more interesting speaker.

Keep up with the news

Keeping up with current events is undoubtedly the best approach to bring up relevant topics throughout any conversation. The subjects don't have to be heavy or need a deep level of knowledge. It's better to know what the hottest songs or videos are, or what the biggest box office hit is, than to be in the dark about what's going on in the world.

Recognise when to shut up

Certain people would rather have no communication at all, particularly in places with limited space, like public transportation. While passing the dull hours on a lengthy flight, you could find it pleasant to chat with the person sitting next to you. However, if that passenger—or others nearby—give you any indications to the contrary, you should assume that your quiet will be regarded as wisdom. In order to avoid becoming sidetracked, make sure you have nothing to read or do to pass the time if you are consistently acting in this manner everywhere you go (and getting bad feedback).

Avoid sharing too much.

Maybe you've come to realise that it's okay to divulge your most private information to complete strangers. After all, you won't see them ever again. Just right? Three problems with this claim:

It's possible that you'll run into them again or meet someone new. It's astonishing how easily your personal secrets may spread in our world of six degrees of separation.

Individuals find it awkward to be aware of another person's private thoughts. Consider yourself as another person's shoes. What if you were to hear someone you hardly knew disclose to you details about their medical issues, romantic relationships, or family disputes?

For you, sharing too much can be a hassle. It's easy enough to ignore the dull daily babbling of our Facebook friends, but a little more difficult to ignore in person.

www.ingramcontent.com/pod-product-compliance
Lightning Source LLC
Chambersburg PA
CBHW050202130526
44591CB00034B/1904